CONFIDENCE SPONSORED BY PAIN

"Strategies and Gifts to Leverage On and Strengthen Your Beliefs"

VENKATESH KRISHNA MURTHY

Published by WOW Book Publishing

Copyright date © Venkatesh Krishna Murthy 2020

ISBN: 9798613451524

All rights reserved. No part of this book may be reproduced in any form or by any electronic or mechanical means including information storage and retrieval systems, without permission in writing from the author.

The purpose of this book is to bring about a change in one's mindset. The views and opinions expressed in this book are that of the author, based on his knowledge acquired and personal experiences.

The author has shared his valuable insights, however, one should validate the same. Apply it, only if he/she feels it is right for them. This is totally based on the decision of the reader, as they should be responsible for their actions.

If you have any comments, questions or suggestions about this book, please do not hesitate to contact the author on:

Email: venkatesh@wharfstreetstrategies.com

You may also follow me on :
LinkedIn: @venkatesh krishnamurthy
Twitter: @venkatesh_wss
Facebook: @strategistentrepreneur
Instagram: @venkatesh_krishna_murthy
Website: www.wharfstreetstrategies.com

DEDICATION

I wrote this book so you, honoured reader leverage on strategies I used in the journey. Perhaps this could bridge the potential gaps, at the moment in your destined journey.

Also, I dedicate this book to enlighten and awaken the warrior inside you. I would want you to experience exercises and understand concepts put in place, to help realise what you are capable of.

Love,

Venkatesh Krishna Murthy

Serial Entrepreneur & International Speaker

CONTENTS

Chapter 1: Why so curious 1

Chapter 2: Powerful mottos to the uninitiated 5

Chapter 3: Darkness as an ally to mould oneself 9

Chapter 4: Well I know my moves were good 13

Chapter 5: The only verdict was not vengeance 18

Chapter 6: I just know the game changers 21

Chapter 7: Peace has nurtured your strength 28

Chapter 8: Victory has partnered with you 32

Chapter 9: Vicissitudes of fate 37

Chapter 10: We simply channelise our gifts 43

ABOUT THE AUTHOR

Venkatesh is a born leader with the same height as Sylvester Stallone, great humour and a charismatic style to showcase enthusiasm for any role he encounters. He is a mastermind who plans his next steps strategically according to the dynamic market while keeping in mind, nuke and corner required to build a successful organisation.

FOREWORD BY VISHAL

Venkatesh has been very dedicated towards completing this book ever since he attended my event. Apart from the fact that this book has an amazing cover, its chapters are very intriguing along with the title. To sum up, he does have an adventurous story, amazing strategy and life changing exercises that could potentially change many lives.

ACKNOWLEDGEMENTS

I acknowledge great souls like Dr. APJ Abdul Kalam for his impactful work, Swami Vivekananda who showcased power of speech and confidence at the World Parliament of Religions. Indeed, they have motivated youth to contribute whilst living their graceful lives.

I am grateful to Vipassana (technique of Buddha) for enlightening me about love and this materialistic life. The teachings of Buddha show us the path of life in a spiritual and selfless aspect.

I acknowledge some great personalities like Sandeep Maheshwari, Edward J C Smith, Tony Robbins, Sadhguru, Gaur Gopal Das, Radhanath Swami, Andy Harrington, Jessen James and Vivek Bindra who have indirectly inspired me to awaken the warrior with their valuable insights for this destined journey.

I am thankful to family, friends, relatives, team in Wharf Street Strategies and Wharf Street Studios for playing their part to support me all along to this point where I finally am launching this book.

I wholeheartedly thank this universe and infinite intelligence for being a driving force all along, giving me the required energy to write this book and also helping me to reach this book out to you, honoured reader.

NOTE TO THE READER

Hello! Hello!

As I respect your time and sincerely wish that you make most of this book, here are a few tips - Once you start reading please remember that each chapter has a story which you can sync into your life, not necessarily in the first or second but surely in one of the 10 chapters. Now there are strategies and concepts, I have mentioned just for you to apply in your life and see how it brings about a difference to you. Yes there are exercises as well, in each chapter or in most need to be done right away, so feel and experience a change in your mindset.

A sincere humble request is that as I believe in giving as much as I can so when you benefit somehow small or big from this book, kindly share the relevant strategy or exercise so others who are in need will feel grateful to you for doing that. Trust me these life changing experiences come back at some point in manifold ways, you cannot even imagine. Keep Sharing and Stay Blessed!

Chapter 1

WHY SO CURIOUS

Something cold sliding down the cheeks while I lay still in the dark and I rub it off and there is a slow voice saying, "Its Ok", but now it pours all over the cheek and nose is flooded. I calm myself down and wonder about the one thing that is known to be the solution to everything. The one thing everyone talks about, the one thing everyone admires, and I'd say the one thing everyone lives for and that includes myself as I didn't have it.

    I wake up and the day repeats and the situation hasn't changed from the previous night and years pass by. I kept craving on how I can achieve the one thing and get as much of it to change this situation. Lost in this thought not knowing how to get the one thing, as everyone is fighting for it makes me feel like I am very ordinary and maybe I don't deserve it. However, there is a sign of perseverance with required hard work to reach that point. The next moment I find myself motivated to impress others and hold a chain ready to go for a physical fight. Then comes along a simple suggestion of words from a close friend about how I could become something fearful giving an impact to those who love me. This took a turn at that point when I was still in a world of infatuation.

    The phase of acrobatic movements to create a diversion from all that was going around did pave a way to another world of illusion.

The competition involved, and the enthusiasm supplemented by a smile of victory became my cup of tea for a while. Exploring the unexplored with a motto of doing something different just because very few were up for it gave me a sense of satisfaction. But at that point I felt it was in vain, as the knowledge acquired at this point seemed redundant. I was simply not aware of its application. Hence, convinced by this situation the one thing which is 'Money' came in small and I took it believing this is all I deserve.

Sustaining at native place despite the congestion of people led to a further compromise. Again, that's what I deserved was my belief. Now the point where a question arose on implementing what was taught for 22 long years in the current nature of work did not resonate or make much sense. The interest in multi-tasking was still prominent at every point, so this led to a venturing passion to learn about India.

Inspired to pursue so called "boring subjects" with a rational perspective eventually landed me nowhere. This is what I believed but honestly this phase was only a stepping ladder to the journey ahead. Here, the tragic part is that I was not being accommodated for any skill which kept me pondering about decisions for having a high risk appetite. Having lost all the access to the one thing, I simply dreamt of putting an end to all of this. However, the subconscious memory enlightened the conscious mind with managerial skills as a choice, this further led me to undertake a course of finance and logistics.

This phase of hardships and transition made me feel lonely despite the fact that I had many followers who admired me at this point for what I was. The interesting interview room for the one thing had a lot of competition and I was mocked at for being the "odd one" in the so-called **rat race**.

> *"When confidence and belief in oneself is 100%, not merely 99.9999% your belief comes true" - VKM*

Lo! My name was called out, I just had to join and start off. Initial days of luxury made it easy for me to accommodate myself in the busy place. There was a challenge again, as I was to head and ensure everything runs smooth and that's when I felt like I was in square one. Yes! hardwork always pays off as it has been the case and I simply remembered to keep working hard. However, the fact that I was being framed for something not exactly my doing literally put me off and I couldn't stay in Mumbai anymore.

Feeling lost and questioning next steps I decided to leave India as I thought it is only known for politics, greed, jealousy and nepotism, so was at least the case where ever I had been. A little hurt but a ray of hope with a new environment revived an urge inside to start afresh with a positive mindset. All the knowledge gained so far was that of an ordinary person and not for an entrepreneur, so I kept working day after day continuously to achieve what was meant for me. Despite being ambitious and supported by family initially I still could not figure out how to get to the destined. I always did have a strong hope and conveyed to the universe, "no matter what happens I am simply going to keep focus on work to enhance skills and I leave the rest for you to take care of".

> *"If god doesn't stop testing then you shouldn't stop fighting, keep going till your resilient fight is acknowledged and the universe joins hands with you" - VKM*

Dear reader, you must realise that life and business always take you upwards and then downwards and back up. This cycle keeps going on at every point and as the buddha says - "stay resilient maintaining a balance at all ends, everything shall pass."

"Improving your resilient nature will help you acknowledge the fact that unpleasant situations are not permanent" - **VKM**

At this point I would like to discuss our understanding of **'GOD and GHOST'**.

We should always remain grateful to this universe whether we succeed or fail. As God is perceived to be someone assumed and created by us. Prayed to for everything and when things go south, he is blamed, that's the irony. Well, we should understand god or infinite intelligence never gave us any assurance or conveyed that we should pray to them to resolve our problem.

Now we need to understand that we live in a world of assumptions!

If you try to understand what a Ghost is, it is a person after death. We assume that its face gets deformed and according to our assumptions, it is meant to hide in secret places like behind doors, closets, under beds all its life and scare as many people it can. This is a bit scary, isn't it? Or is this being a joke, what do you think?

hmmm..never mind this was just my perception!

Chapter 2

POWERFUL MOTTOS TO THE UNINITIATED

Have you noticed that motivation theories from different thinkers are merely read to score marks or used to create supporting theories for a thesis etc. What if these theories can be understood at the grass root level for their meaning and message?

What if they were interpreted to implement them in one's life, that could actually change the mindset of humans. To make one reach their goals in a simpler manner, was the actual motto of these thinkers who wrote these theories. However, the sole purpose is being neglected out here. Hence, curiosity at the start wasn't a gesture out of deliberation, motto is to streamline a mind to the right direction which is of utmost importance.

Now all our lives we keep running on a fixed path, to be successful. Here, we do not realise that each of us have the capability of exploring much more than the rigid path we are following. In the current scenario, if you are going for a desired position and missing out on other areas of interest it will actually take you more time to reach your goal. Some questions asked by closed ones at one point,

Father kept asking "What are you doing exactly? Why won't you listen to elders?",

Some friends "Do you know what you actually want in life, why are you so confused",

Some relatives said "He probably is pursuing some course or must be working hard to make all the money despite his father being rich".

Here the take is, if you have explored various fields in your life it actually won't take you that long to reach your goal as you will experience quite a lot. Hence, the more you learn the more skilled you get. Moreover learning from any source can be applied anywhere to bring about a solution.

Dear reader, here's an exercise I'd want YOU to do right away....

Close your eyes for the next 10 mins, think of all the feedback you have received from others (who have known you for days, weeks, months or years). Please remember to just observe it now as this shouldn't ever impact you again. Slowly acknowledge whatever was said or you've heard,

- If you experience positive energy from any experience - analyse and implement it as soon as possible.
- If you sense negative energy - ignore it with a smile.

Once you have done this first exercise, convey to yourself that feedback from your heart or mind about you being right or wrong, especially when you go to bed is **only what should** matter to oneself. As both have known you since your birth, whatever you have heard from others shouldn't impact you. Simply take what is good and let go of the rest as no feedback can actually impact you unless you react.

It is very usual for you to get judged for your choices in life. At this moment I want you to imagine two trees one very tall like the bamboo tree without branches, reaching the sky and the other one comparatively small in height but branched out and filled with leaves and fruits. Here, both trees are successful with the purpose of their lives as each has achieved what they want to, by choosing different paths. Similarly, you can excel in life with one skill exploring only one area or you can choose multiple paths to be successful. It is you and only you who can know what is required to reach your destination.

For 28 years of life, I believed that the tall tree was destiny. However, for me the short tree with many branches always opened doors to many options and opportunities. Apart from the fact that knowledge enhanced with different subjects, this approach kept me with open arms for further learning. I'd say there is no end to this Christmas tree-like growth. At the end of the day the step that you take and the decision you make based on your validation, leads to an outcome you were destined for.

Dear reader, let me share something that is very entertaining. Whenever you feel low in your life with regard to your career it is pretty obvious that at this point you will attract and come in contact with toxic, low energy people and a negative environment to indulge in wrong habits. Now simply realise that this is simply a bad phase because these people and environment put you further down, could insult or humiliate you for what you are currently. Do not worry, this is actually the best part because on one hand you are hurt but on the other hand you will subconsciously **trigger those emotions (gifts)** which will force or make you take one last risk and do wonders in your life. You must be thinking that I am crazy, right? No, I am not because despite the fact that this happened to me 4 times in life I am still here to share strategies and success stories with you through this book.

Here is another tip, never overthink about anyone because honestly they wouldn't remember what they said in your past and would be the first to congratulate you on your success. So simply live every moment and convey to your mind that it needs to forgive because a prolonged emotion becomes a feeling. This could lead to a problem further leading to frustration which is not healthy.

Also, I have learnt that at the end of the day you don't need courage to hurt, harm or prove anything to others but to forgive someone or accept a reality you need to take such a step as forgiving and accepting really demands a lot of courage. Hence, remember your past with a smile, live right now in confidence with every step which is your purpose and leave the future for the universe as it does it's job really well !!

Chapter 3
DARKNESS AS AN ALLY TO MOULD ONESELF

This was during the years 1988 - 2003, a good 15 long years. My brother wakes me up as he is ready and yeah, it's time for me to jump out into monotony. Kids around are interesting but the teaching doesn't make much sense to me.

Tring   Tring……

That's the bell and I am sad because I need to get back to the actual monotony. I had a feeling of being forced to sit and go on for hours of study, which was not what I wanted for myself but yeah 15 years did condition it well in my head.

This routine kept me at the top in merit, again that was my belief. Supplemented with very good nutrition, I must agree to yum south Indian food by mother. Imagine fruits cut and served in ice cream, dry fruits with milk and yeah, the best part vegetables cut and mixed in yoghurt. I bet all these actually kept me going on. This was a stage where I was like a frog in a well in the comfort zone. Unintentionally limiting exposure due to this situation, but honestly the time when you are most comfortable in life is the time you least expect hardships.

In the year 2004-2005, this phase was full of unprecedented hardships. I, for the first time, left home, caring mother, yum food to pursue education on a land I hardly knew anything about. Here, initially freedom was the claim and I got it in vain. With unknown people, language, and environment came some miscellaneous problems namely, dislocated joints, amoebiasis, madras eye and malaria. However, the nutrition for 15 years fixed them all to some extent. Additionally, the jealous, greedy and egoistic peers messed up my stay with abuses and fights just because I did not belong from their turf apparently. This stage reminds me of the saying "survival of the fittest" as I made it out of this place somehow. Time moved on and so did I.

2012-2013 were the knowledgeable years of life as I got a chance to get familiar with India through UPSC preparations. The hardships in this phase of life was something unimaginable and I was completely lost at this point. Time was hard and energy was not good as I was in the wrong environment wherein I was influenced and misused by people in the north. But while pursuing various subjects of India in a practical manner, made me an open-minded person. However, this felt as if it were all about connecting the dots to get to the destined.

The 100% belief that everything is a learning and is only meant for a bigger cause made me keep my calm. Then it was 2013-2014, here the path of basic shelter chipped in and I took it as I still knew somewhere deep inside that I was meant for something big which I needed to figure out. Leadership and managerial skills kicked in at this point which was unexplored and this gave rise to a stronger and more confident personality, risking it big time by making it somehow. I believe the universe helped me with this leap in life. All the knowledge gained from UPSC preparation was applied here and that gave me temporary success as it was not the destined place. Meanwhile in the year 2014, I called home to gather some support with what I was doing but in vain due to circumstances. So, I made a call to Vipassana (Centre for Buddha's technique) which accepted me and this experience changed my mindset to a different realm altogether. This place felt like all hardships and tears shedded for years were wiped off from life through enlightenment.

Dear reader, I would like to share with you the "Truth about Tears". When you feel like crying, based on intensity with person, thing or place, your pain and experience will be as follows,

- 1 hour of crying, something unexpected that made you a loss (shouldn't have happened) and you start crying.
- 2 hours of crying, based on how much the above meant you extend crying.
- 4 hours of crying, now this could be by relatives where there is jealousy, hatred and backbiting to create misunderstandings. You cry accordingly as it does inflict pain.
- 8 hours of crying, breakup in relationship, betrayal by close friends and being cheated or humiliated by someone you know well. You could get yourself dehydrated while crying.
- 16 hours of crying, means most, that is when treated badly by family or not given importance or required care, support etc and could also include death of any close member. This means a lot and you spend more time crying to relieve your pain.

For pretty obvious reasons you cannot cry more than 16 hours spent in a day. As you need to sleep and this breaks the pattern of your emotions, you simply wander into a different world and are cut-off from miseries of the real world.

Now here is a concept for this chapter - TCOS Quadrant

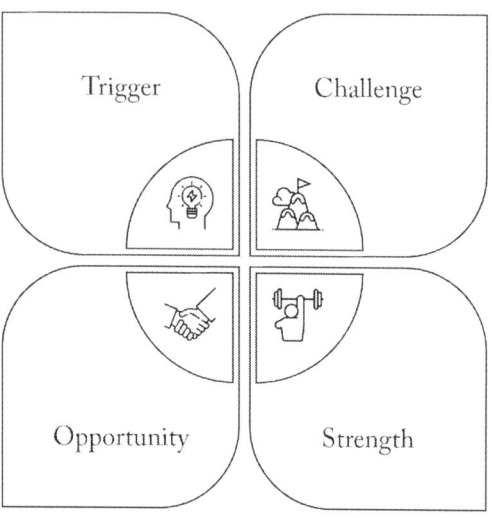

Triggers, are instigated by insults, humiliations and betrayal to shake up the sleeping warrior inside, to awaken and find new strengths.

Challenges, when people or time change there arises a situation for you to handle, outcomes would be based on your steps and decision.

Opportunities, are basically any problem that is spoken about or you encounter in life to open other doors.

Strength, is any feeling, emotion or thought that makes you feel positive and instills confidence.

This quadrant usually focuses on what is needed and not what we are already good at.

Chapter 4

WELL I KNOW MY MOVES WERE GOOD

"Acquired knowledge when implemented appropriately always brings the opportunity to make a big difference" - VKM

10 years ago, I didn't quite know what I was meant for. Before I go into this amazing chapter, I would like to share with you timeline for the past 10 years, so you to relate to the story that follows,

2009: B.Tech Mechanical and IT Dual Engineering in VIT University

2010: Test Analyst at TCS (JPMC Banking and Financial Services)

2012: UPSC aspirant

2014: Finance & Operations #Amity University

2015: Assistant Process Manager Eclerx (Morgan Stanley Commodities Settlements)

2016: Anglia Ruskin University (Supply chain and Bloomberg certification)

2017: Intern in various Fintech, Payment and Blockchain startups

2018: UK Tier 1 Graduate Entrepreneur for company Wharf Street Strategies Limited, into emerging technologies and emerging marketing techniques

2019: Founder of Wharf Street Studios Limited into gaming, mixed reality and animated videos

*"Frustration can penetrate any routine; a breakthrough unleashes the taste of freedom." - **VKM***

After 10 years of hardships while learning, travelling, networking and acknowledging inner self, finally led me to build passionately with a team at WSS. This gave opportunities to mentor and touch the lives of 1000's of aspiring students. As a keynote speaker cherishing the 36 hours Hackertech'19 by Entrepreneurship Cell, VIT made my amazing journey to do much more with a selfless & resilient attitude. Sharing such experiences from all these years can help millennials learn and benefit from this journey, so they unleash their purpose to bring about a difference.

Silicon Valley of India - Bangalore 2010-2011, started working with one of the best IT companies, living in my hometown. Delivering excellence at work, still, something was amiss. Although I was a star performer and a great team member, its relevance to my qualification was arising a question inside me. I had the urge to leave because of politics as it made me stagnant in growth as well. The feeling was further triggered by the death of a 28-year-old cousin as he suffered from cancer and tuberculosis. This incident invoked a realization and I decided to move to the North in mid 2011 to explore career and liaise with different cultures. I always had a feeling I was meant for something big.

Capital of India - Delhi 2011-2012, instilled an innocent thought of handling goons with official power, made me join UPSC. But at that moment I didn't realise that the purpose of this knowledge is to take me far on my journey to reach the destined. Born and brought up in a foreign land never gave me an opportunity to know about India and I wanted to learn its potential. While preparing for UPSC my inner voice got stronger with every passing day that this knowledge would come handy in future in some form. With a pinch of salt in my journey the judgemental voices never left my side "he is ruining his life", "he is not sure what he wants", "he is nothing without his father". However, I kept focussed and believed in myself.

Financial Capital of India - Mumbai 2015-2016, accepting the unexpected, the feeling of bouncing back gave me peace of mind for quite some time. This time I was not a team member but had a team from whom I had to learn and then manage. However much to my disappointment the MNC culture was pretty much the same politics. The jealous and egoistic peers made a negative environment which made me regret my decision. Again, this was further triggered with the death of a 52-year-old uncle from a heart attack and it did impact me as I was attached to him since childhood. Again, I just left without thinking of what was going to happen next.

Financial Hub of the world - London 2017-2018, exploring the toughest market in the world. Moving to this place of opportunities and challenges kept me excited but I didn't have a clue how exactly I would leverage on onboarding these opportunities. I was shunned down with all the knowledge and experience gathered for 28 long years. But the urge to learn, the acceptance to humiliation and insults made me prone to them, create strengths and take up and leverage on gifts in hand already. But life is not easy, those I assumed to be well-wishers betrayed me diplomatically. I was helpless again, all that I built in this one year was taken away at a snap.

Dear reader, always remember one thing, life and business work like a trading graph where there is growth and decline. It is at this point that you acknowledge your quality of resilience and skill of observing. When there is a decline simply remember the moment when the idea popped into your mind and how you felt about it back then. Here, all you need to do is believe in it the same way you did at that point, work on it again and you will see it growing again. Basically when your mind firmly believes in the idea, your graph goes up. When you bring in excuses and reasons or limitations due to family etc that's when you will witness a down graph.

So coming to our next exercise, this is the first and ongoing

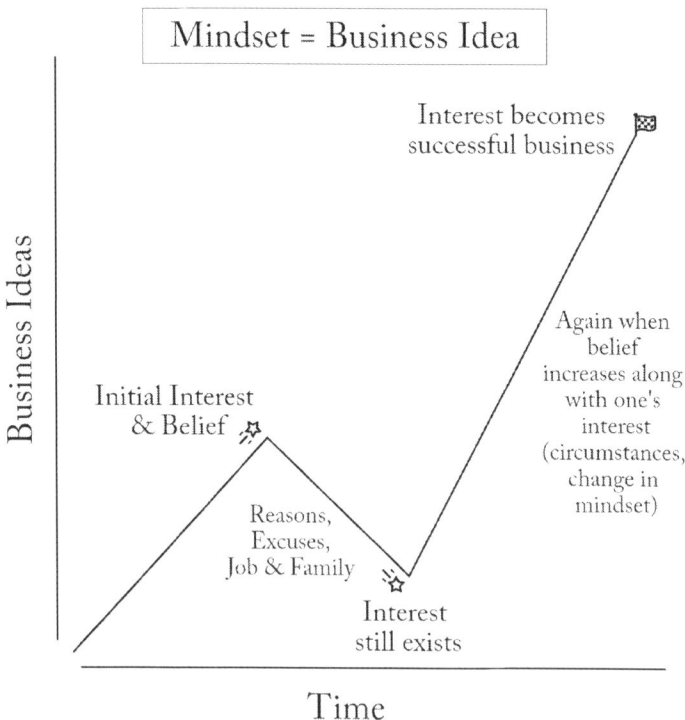

step to being an Entrepreneur which is to 'Believe in Oneself'. I would want **You** - honoured reader of this book is to do the below exercise right away,

1. Close your eyes for 10 mins and think of all the people, you felt have so called "betrayed, insulted, humiliated and underestimated" you.

2. Focus on all that they have said or done to you and attract all those feelings and emotions you faced at that point. Simply observe your situation at that point (a good deep breath), go into each moment one by one, do this for 2 mins.

3. Now channelise all that energy to your mind and activate it, then release your deep breath by forgiving all of them wholeheartedly and know it's true in this very moment.

This exercise every morning before you start your day, will trigger your purpose in life again giving it meaning and would keep you alive every minute. This can bring changes within and around yourself. I have shared this only because it worked for me and I wholeheartedly wish it works for you as well.

> *"Life is not a course to be pursued, it is a feeling to experience in your present" - VKM*

Chapter 5

THE ONLY VERDICT WAS NOT VENGEANCE

The year 2005-2007 always kept me motivated with a bunch of girls around and a gang to take care of, in case the situation demands. I didn't want to have the same experience as I had in the past 2 years, so I increased my responsibility. With this came a sense of satisfaction from a close friend, supporting me to take up another course in university making me feel unique.

In 2008-2009 the will to perform a group dance in front of 2000 people was something wonderful. Again, teaming up with other friends to battle online was an amazing diversion from what I was previously doing. Learning to drive a bike and then a car apart from placement were some takeaways during this phase I'd say.

Well this was a great learning phase because I actually felt that beating up people is how I can contribute and change this planet, but later realised though this was followed at home it was not the right path. Soon I felt the right path was to clear UPSC to become a bureaucrat and use a gun to eliminate so called bad as this would be legal. Again, Vipassana (Centre for Buddha's technique) made me realize in October 2014 that this was also not the right path. This is the era to change the mindset of people to bring about a difference. Power is in mindset and not in anything else.

However, one must remember that the mind is your best friend and could be your only possible enemy to manipulate your emotions at times, creating a destructive emotion called anger. This is very much different from hunger which comes naturally and cannot be controlled. Yes! Anger can be fine tuned and a simple way I figured out to tackle the same, took years to be honest.

Dear reader, right now please set a reminder in your mind that whenever you lose yourself you just need to start by cleaning your cupboard, table and chair. So here's what you do when you lose your mind or get frustrated or angry and you cannot calm yourself down,

- Quickly leave for a haircut or trim your hair, armpits and shave your beard etc your mind is diverted, then cut your nails and start to clean your room.

- Now quickly change, go for a jog and take a shower in lukewarm water. Your energy instantly changes if you notice.

- Then sit down, take 10 deep breaths and think about your goal in 2020. Imagine yourself discussing ideas and brainstorming with interested friends and family. Keep your eyes closed and do this for 10 mins. (*Soon in life you will notice the universe sending similar mindset people and individuals who think the same way).

- Take 10 deep breaths now as you visualise your dream, also imagine yourself giving talks on social media channels, interviews with well known people and at the end of the day you are free to imagine all possibilities for your growth based on your situation.

When you feel or witness a "destructive emotion" always

imagine and believe in a constructive cause (goal) of your life, which will serve as an antidote in this situation. Inform, convey and imbibe this into your mind that there is no one who has actually scaled up the ladder without hardships and you need to keep reminding yourself that you are on the same path as them. It's just like if you open or scroll to the middle of a movie you might witness trouble created by the villains but if you go to the end of the movie (which I usually do) you will find there is always a happily ever after. Now you must tell yourself that at the end the mist will clear and you will be good as nothing on this planet is permanent not even time, not you and not even your situation.

Do this exercise as it should be applicable, as you are reading this book and see how this changes things for you in a week's time.

So reader here is another tip, if you are a chain smoker or into any other addiction this takeaway is for you. Have you noticed that if you visit a grocery store after having your meals you tend to purchase less when compared to what you would purchase with an empty stomach. Here's a tip in case you are a chain smoker, simply take 10 long deep breaths whenever you feel like smoking, after that you can have a smoke. Now this habit rooting from the desire to smoke wherein you smoke 2 cigarettes, overtime will reduce to 1 with this exercise. Also, you will notice this very desire to fade away eventually.

> *"Any habit done only we want to and not when the habit wants us to, simply showcases self-control"* - **VKM**

Chapter 6

I JUST KNOW THE GAME CHANGERS

In 2018-2019, the quality of multiplying risk with confidence kicked in and I did it again. Honestly, all the experience and network gained in a year was required to streamline the company www.wharfstreetstrategies.com, for which I was sponsored. Now, I didn't just build one, rather 2 companies this time and both kicked off big time. Overtime company services increased and so did products, along with strategic alliances. So let me share in this chapter, what it takes to run a company. Not just theory but this has been a great experience in the past 2 years.

Apart from the experience in investment banking I expanded with some skill sets that I acquired while creating this path for these 2 companies. I would like to highlight them as below,

1. Creating, editing and formatting valuable content.
2. Working on wireframes and designs.
3. Greenfield and brownfield projects for Emerging technologies.
4. Emerging marketing techniques with advanced tools.
5. Pitching and Liaising for various products and services to clients.
6. Optimizing usage of funds.

7. Dedicated marketing campaigns for customer/user acquisition.
8. Striking strategic partnerships with lucrative deals as a win-win situation.

At this point apart from imparting above acquired skills to team, I wanted to onboard leaders and wasn't looking for employees. Leaders who can take responsibility and care for others to make a difference to this planet.

Dear reader, remember what worked for someone doesn't necessarily have to work for you, as you need to create your own path. Let us take an example to understand it more, if you blindly listen or follow some rich or so called successful people on this planet who were school dropouts. You will notice they may blame the schooling system for not teaching about money that wouldn't be totally justified as they never experienced school. Also the former fail to understand that school is only meant to imbibe discipline in one's life and this ingrained habit would take us a long way further.

Well, I'd say this is how it worked in my case and if you had your schooling then leverage on what you got from it. Than listening to the aforementioned who haven't been in school and are yet successful, as what worked for them need not work for you. I would like to highlight that it is one's sole decision to go to school or drop out. Blindly other people's footsteps cannot be followed to reach your destiny, as you need to make your own prints.

One more thing I noticed in all the travel around is that people keep many opinions about other personalities. Definitely one has all the freedom to keep opinions and pass their personal judgments about any country, culture, economy, politicians, and bureaucrats. However, in such a scenario you should remember that before passing comments on their doings. One should learn by traveling to many places around the globe, reading history, interacting with people and learning about different cultures.

If your thought process is confined by staying at just 2 or 3 different places for your entire life, and your only source of knowledge is newspapers, fun magazines, social media and different sources of internet then you should give a thought about your comments. The point I am making here is that one should have enough experience and witness both sides of the story. As seeing it from one side and deciding wouldn't give a holistic picture. Comments passed for the sake because the majority are doing it, will only keep you in the crowd and stagnant your growth.

Let's discuss the leader and the boss?? Yes, I guess, however, let's discuss something very interesting about them, the unique difference is that the former works like green tea to ensure consistency and maintain passion, the latter works like coffee to get work done at the nick of time and then motivation disappears. In simple words, the former doesn't simply motivate people but makes his people realise the truth about themself which is based on a long term relation perspective. Now the latter believes in motivation wherein he just wants temporary results. A leader is like an entrepreneur who works for passion and vision and a boss works like a businessman for profits and mission!

So reader, ready to learn something interesting?

Noticed that people look out for companies that are recession proof or for a well settled career. However, the below steps will help you become recession proof to lead others,

- Make a list of all the influential people you know, pick a conversation with them to change your mindset and environment.

- Start writing about what you have done in the past week and what you will do this week, repeat this every monday morning. Create a business plan for which I have given guidelines later in this chapter.

- Work 15*7*365 that is on weekends, day and night when ever needed till you feel burnt out. Ensure you give 2 hours to yourself and 7 hours of sleep.

- Hire a trusted and passionate person who believes in your vision and is willing to help you, this will make your belief stronger and you will feel responsible. Remember your people are your family for your vision.

- Take no holidays for years together meaning cut your parties and celebrations temporarily and work as if it were any normal day. As it is your passion, you can work at your will as it interests you.

- Add as much value you can to yourself acquiring knowledge and speak about your idea while working on strategic alliances and expansions for business development be it big or small.

- Learn to spend every single penny from your pocket to make this run as if you don't spend you block the flow of money and cannot expect others to spend on you or your idea.

> *"Give up the pleasant part of your life so you can live a life others only dream of." - **VKM***

Let's not stop for a ceremony now......

Dear reader, get ready with a paper and pen to bring out your business plan, the first step is close your eyes, think of your childhood, teenage life, etc. Now simply think of every decade you lived that is 1-10, 11-20, 21-30 years and so forth. At some point there must have been a thought or a feeling you had deep inside that you have always wanted to do. This could be anything with art, coding, science, design basically whatsoever interests you. Simply remember this could be anything random but let me tell you in the next 15 mins you will have your business plan, how cool is that?

> *"It's never too late to start and bring out our hidden potential and become what we are meant to be." – VKM*

The first step of your idea to become a reality is putting it into existence by writing it on a paper. Let's do a quick exercise!

When we talk about building an idea, one thing that adds up to the list of activities is a 'Pitch Deck'. Now, pitch deck is a presentation that entrepreneurs use to showcase their business. It includes a brief about the business idea, problems faced and how it can be solved, your target audience, product and market position, etc. Always keep in mind the above points while creating it, here are some specifics.

- Keep things simple but make them engaging.
- What you create in the next 30 mins should be presentable in 3-4 mins. So investors can understand the crux, to ask questions and discuss valid points after you present it to them.
- From past experiences I analysed that investors are concerned about product competition, its market and scalability as well.

- The flow of the presentation is important so that information is in sync.
- Problem/ Opportunity - write about a problem faced and find an opportunity in that space (*any problem solved makes money).

Let's start - pen down whatever comes to your mind for the below points right away (do not worry about the content at this point)

1. **Introduction** (what your business idea does in real-time)
2. **Solution** (timing of business idea as to why it is needed now)
3. **Market Size and Validation** (include information, statistics and facts to strengthen your business).
4. **Product** (practical application of your business, include videos for a visual impact)
5. **Competition** (analyse the market to showcase competition and your Unique Selling Proposition)
6. **Comparability Analysis** (evaluate your idea based on growth of other companies in the same domain)
7. **Financials** (A basic flow of cash with profit and a pie-chart to showcase percentage split)

[*Hint** Profit = Revenue - Sales - Expenses]

Keep everything to the point and this presentation should be max 8-10 slides only. Do not worry about content in the first shot. Give it sometime but at least at this point you have the first draft of your business plan.

Now as we have accomplished the first tangible step towards achieving your goal. Let me give you some tips, put yourself into the shoes of your users and,

- Position your audience
- Highlight the problem faced
- Give a promising solution
- Position yourself when you faced this problem (to bring the connect)
- Give a tip on how it helped you and will help other users

When you think on these lines, you will be able to sync in and showcase your solution identified, to be worthy in the market. And this entire dedicated 30 mins will help you to think like an entrepreneur to start off with.

Chapter 7

PEACE HAS NURTURED YOUR STRENGTH

Well heard that the mind isn't just wandering but has a state it reaches as part of enlightenment. The intelligence coming from it does not necessarily need to be used to manipulate people and situations, or to find out if anyone else is doing the same.

Now, we all keep wondering what we are living for and at times get bored of doing things for ourselves too. We crave for more success and have an aversion to our failures along with building attachments to this materialistic world. This leads to suffering and we get stuck in the vicious cycle of misery. I remember picking up the phone to call 'mother' to get home as I couldn't handle things anymore. Unfortunately, I was denied and this broke me down further. However, I made a call to Vipassana and they took me in.

Now we do take out time for people claiming work of some sort, visit places and enjoy time with friends. Well wouldn't it be worthwhile to give just 11 days of our life to enlightenment and learn about god, religion, life, death, suffering? What do all of these mean? What is our true purpose and what is "I", "me"?

People in Vipassana strive to provide nutritious food, accommodation and shelter for free in today's world, where one might not think of helping others even for a day. They communicate teachings so politely and just want you to learn this technique, without any expectations. What does it mean to become pure in body and mind and why is it important to spread and share your knowledge to help others who are in search of peace and happiness, which lacks big time in this century.

It so happened all my life that the Deity of home, Sai Baba was all I could see around me in shops, houses etc. After Vipassana I could see Gauthama Buddha wherever I went, not just houses etc but even in books. This is when I understood that it is all in the mind. This works in a similar manner with the person you love most be it your girlfriend, mother, brother, sister and father etc. Your mind finds features of that gender you love with the gender you meet and tries to sync them and you miss the aforementioned accordingly.

Dear reader, let me tell you the truth about "Love". Most of us confuse ourselves by saying my house, my father, my car, my brother, my laptop, my child etc. Have you noticed something here? The word my is "misery as an attachment" if you think about it and acknowledge this fact and remind your mind that it is a house, father, car, brother, laptop. Feed this to your mind that nothing is permanent as nothing belongs to you, it will make you feel much lighter in life. Bear in mind you don't have to disown or do anything you just need to remind your mind, rather communicate it repeatedly so your mind knows the truth.

As a matter of fact, you should close your eyes right now and think about these 3 below in quotes:

"When there is no person, place, thing or situation (memory) on this planet that you hate, then you experience Love"

"When you experience this unconditional Love selflessly with no expectations, ready to sacrifice and forgive you can feel enlightenment within and around you"

"Attachment with parents, emotions with loved ones, affection from friends, desires of the body are temporary in nature. We just need to remind ourselves about this truth which will simplify life for us reducing unwanted stress and anxiety".

In fact if you do this exercise you will notice your ability to solve and handle situations and people in a much more effective manner. Well I have preached the same and it worked for me, so you should give this a try and validate what I am saying. As you are my honoured reader and I value your time for reading this book. I wholeheartedly want you to benefit as much once you finish reading this book and that's the reason I have kept this book small and to the point so it creates an impact and makes a difference to this planet !!

Now let us look into one more interesting aspect of assumptions, imagine a river between two banks having people on both sides and the person cleaning the pond on one side notices that people on the other side of the bank are polluting the river. This person feels that it is useless to try as he is all alone fighting for a noble cause and looks around to find none other than him with the same motto. One day he walks alongside the river bank and sees that at one place there are so many people cleaning the river on one side while there is hardly anyone polluting the river on the other side. It is simple when you are in search of people with good intentions and you preach what is good as well, you will realise that good are no less in number and the same applies on the contrary too.

All our lives we keep assuming that the world is full of bad people so let me tell you a story here. While I was pursuing a career as an engineer I met loads of engineers or I thought I did. Once I started working as a manger most of the contacts were managers. I kept wondering subjects like art, singing, environmentalists and miscellaneous paths pursued which looks vague to me, should hardly have any scope as there are not many doing the same. However, the true fact is in a particular time period what you are and what you think, you simply tend to attract similar minds in a huge number be it any profession or belief system.

At this point I would like to highlight the fact that when you need advice or help you should take, follow, preach the person who has already done it. Not from someone who is in the same situation as you. For example, if you want to be a great entrepreneur you shouldn't take advice from a person doing a job hope that makes sense. You can relate the same in other circumstances.

I am sharing all learnings through life experiences and thoughts in mind, so that all readers can derive benefits from the same in some manner or the other. Saving some time for their mind-boggling thoughts on unwanted assumptions giving them clarity. Dear readers, this chapter is a little deep, you might want to give it another shot to be clear on what I have communicated. Trust me this will be worthwhile doing so, go for it !!

*"When you start believing you start realizing, this realization imbibes the needed change, once this change becomes evident, you start witnessing what you always wanted to" - **VKM***

Chapter 8

VICTORY HAS PARTNERED WITH YOU

This chapter is a dear one, as it showcases that part of the journey where I became an entrepreneur and was recognized in the UK. As I always had a vision to start a digital technology firm and create a work environment where people have freedom to explore their skills without fear. I knew deep down that I still need to understand some core concepts, as starting a business is not easy when it comes to managing it.

Now coming from an investment banking background, I decided to pursue supply chain management as next career step in the year 2016. Anglia Ruskin University (ARU) was offering the same along with access to the Bloomberg terminal, which was an added advantage for me. Supply Chain Management (SCM) gives an overview on how to deliver a product or service to customers efficiently. SCM also teaches one how to ensure quality when running a business for a product or service. The practical approach in our course subjects alongside placement year had a significant impact on career perspective. It taught me to implement learning from classroom sessions.

I'd say that experience with ARU was worthwhile as I was guided by the friendly staff out there, regarding every aspect crucial for a student's progress. The teaching and support staff gave a fruitful experience indeed. As the pragmatic approach with course subjects led to enhancements with analytical skill sets.

As mentioned in earlier chapters, I would just touch upon placement year as a business consultant with various fintech and blockchain start-ups. Here, I learned crucial aspects of operations, technology, marketing, staffing, management and strategies required to set up a firm from scratch. The most significant benefit was that this placement opened doors to opportunities as I outperformed tasks. While doing so other business start-ups in the market noticed this and approached me to assist them in their businesses. Yes, there were quite many challenges as most tasks and activities I performed were very new to me when assigned by each start-up. But they believed in my potential to give them the best possible outcome and I made that true by giving my best.

The journey with ARU didn't stop here as they continuously assisted and supported me morally at every step to make my dream come true, sponsored a Tier 1 Graduate Entrepreneur Visa to start a technology and digital marketing firm www.wharfstreetstrategies.com as I always wanted to. I am highly obliged to ARU for bestowing this opportunity onto me, as it paved an amazing pathway to link studies with placement.

You might want to check out the blog created by the university to honour my success, https://aru.ac.uk/blogs/venkatesh-story

Dear reader, belief is very important for one to thrive in today's world. Acquiring knowledge is good but understanding what you read and see, importantly interpreting information to implement it accordingly is the need of hour.

- If people say you are overconfident, you need to believe you have a positive mindset.

- If they call you egoistic you need to believe you have self-respect that is with what you have learnt and applied.

- Jealousy should never crop up inside anyone, instead if you feel ashamed and trigger this thought "if he can, then I should as well". All this will help you progress in life.

> *"Success after you fear, maybe true but remember the fearless have nothing to do with success or failure, they simply keep progressing at their pace." - VKM*

Dear reader, if you've noticed, questioning is the nature of human existence, which can be changed into realistic answers if used as an opportunity. However, these questions can make one overthink and shake one's confidence to overtake their belief system. Some people question the existence of god. However, if someone said do you believe in your breath the answer is always a Yes! So here is another exercise,

1. Sit down on a chair and raise your hands up, now bring in the air element inside through your nose down into your stomach and breathe out by bringing your hands down. Do this movement 10 times and feel the energy pumping in and out.

2. Then rest your hands on your lap, calm yourself down to a comfortable position and liaise with yourself, feeling the positivity around at this moment.

3. Observe the state of your mind it could be in a notorious state, adult state or monster state, now this could possibly happen because of your situations or circumstances.

4. Slowly place both your palms on your head and keep reminding your mind that it is ok and kindly do not conflict with your mind for any reason at this moment whatsoever.

5. Slowly while you observe, connect yourself with your mind. Remember this will take some time as all your life you have been instructed by your mind and now it is the other way round.

6. Build a rapport with your mind and pass or convey a positive message to your mind that no matter what the situation is, what the state it is in right now that you totally accept that state of your mind and tell this to your mind impactfully, thankfully and gratefully.

7. Your mind is always your best friend and could possibly be your enemy, now is the time to speak to your mind and bring it to a neutral state. Bond with it by thanking it gratefully for everything it has done for you and convey that you are always with your mind.

8. Now thank your mind for everything it has done so far be it good or bad, thank it repeatedly and be as much grateful you can to your mind for its decisions as that's the reason why you sit here in this place today. Do this for 2 minutes.

9. Think of 2 events in the past 2 years be it so called "good or bad" but have helped you to get to where you are and again thank your mind for making those decisions for you. Do this for 2 minutes and spend a min on each event.

10. Think of 2 people in the past 2 years who have done so called "good or bad" to you and forgive them wholeheartedly. Know and acknowledge this is true at this moment.

11. Now let's believe for the next 2 minutes that you are living a blissful life with no materialistic expectations where you do not crave for money, property or any other luxuries in life. Imagine everything you do is totally out of passion. Imagine you being involved in it without focusing on the results, this could be anything you always wanted to do. Do this for the next 2 minutes and importantly be in the moment.

Once you finish this slowly open your eyes at your own pace. I bet you feel great, so simply do this at least twice a week.

Here is a quote for you,

> *"If your technique is really genuine, everyone irrespective will join to follow the same" - **VKM***

Chapter 9
VICISSITUDES OF FATE

All the knowledge gained in life was proliferated by working with start-ups. It gave me a whole new level of responsibilities. Here there was no way of blaming others for the things done, as everybody is responsible for each activity. From October 2017 to March 2018 every project I was involved with, required different kinds of expertise wherein experience and education played an important role. The journey with all projects has been very exciting yet challenging. Building projects from scratch is a challenge, I was associated with the top notch who work to convert an idea into reality.

Working with different people from different cultural backgrounds and countries was challenging, as tasks had to be coordinated and delivered on time. I had to manage time zones accordingly with the team in every project to ensure these timelines. Sometimes prejudice and expectation of culturally different people created hurdles for me as it lead to false assumptions. This affected work adversely as people see things as they want to see and miss to see the bigger picture. Nevertheless, as an achiever I was able to complete tasks as per plan. Education and course played an important role in managing different situations thrown at me at different points in time.

Here, I was not limited to performing tasks that were assigned or expected out of me, instead I was involved in every other activity beyond. Be it pitching at events, conducting meetups, creating a marketing plan, helping the platform/app to be launched and strategic expansion to other countries. However, the experience I gained taught me the value of hard work, ownership and self-sustainability and gave the feel of becoming recession-proof.

Dear reader, remember the time I said "when you are most comfortable you don't expect hardships or unpleasant situations." At this point time was challenging but I had hope with a way to showcase and use skills, but in vain as outcomes were taken away from me. Let me walk you through this journey which gave me a final push to the destined path,

October 2017, was when placement commenced on a positive note with a fintech company. I started the journey to entrepreneurship, time was pretty hard with unexpected situations which is the case of a start-up. I had to tackle situations on a bold note as this was an undying zeal towards passion.

This was a point where I struck deals and planned on partnering with companies to expand, participated in roadshows. Events played an important role wherein we could showcase our idea to reputed firms and got noticed by quite a few who approached us themselves for the same.

Another activity which came up, was into developing games and mobile applications on a global level. We went that extra mile to create banner designs, posters and ads which were necessary for marketing campaigns.I was learning from everyone around. So, the first month was imbibed with rigorous training and an intense desire to help others & meet their goals. Also, hard work and dedication proved fruitful as I could showcase experience and knowledge to a huge audience.

November 2017, travelling as and when required kind of made months pass unnoticed for me. This month I struck a strategic partnership deal after research and thereon was associated with responsibilities not limited to just managing operations, technology, finance but also to handle web development, token economics, etc to create database management. Later this month came **Epiko Regal**, a game of dreams to represent cultural heritage. I have researched and worked day and night since 2017 for the same. The journey so far with this project has been really exciting, as it gave me deep insights of how the game industry works in the UK and around the world. At this moment, the game is in a development phase where the initial build for the same is ready to test that is a **proof of concept (POC)**. The best part is we created www.wharfstreetstudios.com with a team of warriors who have been completely involved to give our community one of the best experiences of entertainment in 2020.

December 2017, everything from the past two months kicked in an amazing growth with career, bringing exposure to the world of emerging markets and entrepreneurship. It thus gave me a feeling to revolutionize scope in various business fields. I believe that everything is connected to the service industry wherein one can research and thus leverage strengths of different companies to work out an ecosystem. Provided this is done diligently and managed properly, it is an achievable task.

January 2018, new year, I started working in project

management further expanding knowledge in the same as per client requirements. At this point we hired new interns to delegate some tasks. This helped me big-time and I am always thankful to them for supporting me with their smart & intelligent play.

February 2018, we onboarded a project sync. which is very dear to me. The founder has amazing design skills and innovations. While working on the same I personally found it to be a very challenging project not because of the kind of tasks that were assigned. But during this project one of the developers left the project due to stress at the last moment and the whole project could have got delayed, somehow things were managed at the last minute.

The beauty of work is when it gives you challenges, we have to be quick enough to find solutions. With quick decisions I was able to pull off the project and deliver it on time meeting deliverables. This project taught me that it is not necessary for one to always work in a comfortable environment. Sometimes one has to go that extra mile to work in favour of his team. We handled web development, making it mobile responsive and also managed their bounty campaign. This project was said to be unachievable with the time left to complete all these tasks but with perseverance we were able to deliver accordingly.

P.S. **Bounty campaigns** are an integral part of digital marketing to promote the enterprise, thus we organized social media bounties, article bounties, etc.

March 2018, here I was active with the community members & provided them progress updates to bridge the gap between different organizations and the participants. With this placement was coming to an end and I was planning on how I could leverage on the Tier 1 Graduate Entrepreneur Visa. The process started in April wherein I wanted to onboard all above companies as clients to start www.wharfstreetstrategies.com

Now these 6 months were probably the craziest and the busiest times of life. I was running all over the place for projects by taking on a range of activities including finance, marketing, customer service and technology support for operations and process management. Having said that business analytics and strategic planning enabled a wider scope to reflect and link work activities to course study modules with Anglia Ruskin University. To sum up I demonstrated myself diligently, even weak points were converted to strengths with this perseverance. The final outcome of this phase was adapting and understanding work culture, team management and individual responsibility as a leader to build an organization.

I believe doing something different and unique is possible, only when your appetite for taking a risk is big and you leverage as much on credit from your sources. Believing your decisions further builds your confidence and I did this in a very short span of time.

Dear reader, here is the strategy of this chapter, learn about various companies and how they can leverage on the other - find out what is missing or is needed in each of these companies. Identify where one company can benefit the other and complement what is missing.

For example, If you analysed 6 companies perse, then maybe **company 5** misses something that can be bridged or fulfilled by **company 1** and that's how you can strike a deal on leverage !

Before I end this chapter I would like to end this with some enlightenment by asking yourself 6 questions,

1. Does anything actually belong to you here in this life? *hmmm..*
2. Can you be cheated or betrayed? *Think well before you answer a yes to this question (Hint : That's not possible if the first question is a No)*
3. What is right and wrong? *Ask yourself, is everything taught by your parents and teachers in your childhood so called "right"? Things they haven't told you of and you haven't experienced yet are they "wrong"*
4. What is good and bad? *Any task or activity that makes your mind pleasant is good (P.S. if it makes you feel good temporarily then you need to rethink). The vice-versa of this bad.*
5. Why are you actually doing what you are doing right now? *I just wish you realised the answer to this question. Ask yourself deep inside (end result of working to earn? just to pass this on to your next generation?)*
6. Can you live a life just for others, apart from just your bloodline? *(Hint : The answer lies within and this book is the catalyst for you to realise the same)*

"When the storm hits hard, simply HOLD, STAY and SURVIVE but do not leave, when it clears life will progress again" -
VKM

Chapter 10
WE SIMPLY CHANNELISE OUR GIFTS

3 years ago I came to London and realised that all I had learnt since 28 years wasn't applicable, this left me wondering how that was the case. I'd say only or less than 0.01% people understand about gifts and that every person has gifts within. By gifts I mean any kind of ability, skill, experience, knowledge, talent or expertise that they imbibed or gained over time.

It was at this point that I started this journey from an off-license store and later in a souvenir shop, as I kind of believed what people in London advised me. Now it did strike mind at a point that if we need to do something big we need to risk it all, so I wanted to be a trader. I borrowed money from a friend while working and traded in commodities which was my line and made a good return. After that I believed in gifts and took a vow to never do odd jobs which I wasn't meant for and wanted to start something by myself. However, for a business I had to work with multiple start-ups to find out what was needed for me to begin with. Unfortunately after a year I was taken off the main companies I invested in, raised funds for and partnered with as they felt they didn't require me anymore and I was all broken down.

I remember I woke up one morning in July 2018 and head was heavy, I was not able to think about what would happen next as I felt like now I am nowhere. This kept on going for quite a few days until the warrior inside spoke to me saying "Hey you know something, you built everything for them right? Do you realise in the process you acquired every skill required in almost every domain for a startup? Why don't you just start from scratch as you just did for them"?

Dear reader, I am sure you can relate to this warrior I am talking about and yes that's when I decided to start all over again. Now here is the thing, I simply put down all skills and services I provided to these companies and created a workable business model claiming that I have provided these services to them. I showcased every acquired skill in this model, required for a start-up.

P.S. remember when you break down at any point for any reason and no one believes in you, go and speak to yourself in the mirror and say "I can and I will do it again", do it everyday as it will put you up as you just need one person to believe in you to start off and that's the person in the mirror. I'd like to add something here as it is a part of this concept, if you ever felt at some point when everyone's around and you still get lost, felt this way?? Yes, that's loneliness. Again this is one exercise that will help you from depression big time and you will never feel lonely again !!

Keep doing this and give your best until you hear one real - time voice saying "wow, your passion is amazing and you will get to heights". That's it ! eventually the number of voices will multiply which will in turn boost your confidence and you merge with a belongingness to this universe.

> *"This is not the time when you visit the psychiatrist dear reader, simply remember the psychiatrist cannot solve your problem as 40% of his mind is always occupied with his problems for which he needs to visit another co-psychiatrist. In short, the warrior and the solution lies within !!"* - **VKM**

Let me be honest here, the biggest reason for success is not qualification but I would say it is communication and confidence that came from accumulating knowledge over time. As I say this I would like to talk about "Effective Communication in an organisation" that I applied as well. How can we not notice something that is so crucial to an organisation??

You must have heard that communication needs to be done in the right manner without which it would never be effective. But effective communication would keep an organisation and any relationships intact. By this I mean your message needs to be conveyed at the right time to the right person and yes in the right situation. Now the same rule might not work on some, hence it should be dynamic according to the situation.

This step if not done correctly, could possibly lead to the demise of your organisation and here's the thing if you don't build a good rapport among peers your organisation could simply fall apart as it would lead to misunderstandings, communication gaps and create stress in the organisation, Yes?

That's why effective communication is the key to success, be it in your personal and professional life as it will always help them maintain an environment in harmony. Let me tell you what I mean by this, for an organisation to be successful we need to convey appropriate messages to the concerned person at the right time, also this should be based on the situation. You need to brainstorm, analyse then discuss this with the concerned person when you witness a communication gap. You should gather the courage to discuss this in person and then **Email** appropriately to convey things as written communication keeps you on the same page. Now you must be wondering what is so great I have heard or read this, that's the point we only feel amazed when we read and hear things but we don't take actions and when we act, it is not done in the right manner.

For example, sometimes people say we need to sort things out immediately when another person reacts weirdly and should warn him/her. I simply tell them to observe the situation and analyze what needs to be done because he/she might not be in the right state of his/her mind. One should not react when they notice anger and negativity increasing, simply wait for the right moment once he/she is back to the normal state. I believe everyone, as humans could lose their cool at some point and that's very normal or it's just that I am pretty cool about it. Because this worked to keep my organisation intact I wanted to share the same and you can imagine how challenging it could be while implementing this among 17 minds to keep a harmonious environment. But it is worth considering as your people will feel motivated and the environment becomes positive in the company as well. And yes, this doesn't have to work 100% but would mitigate misunderstandings and build a bond. Trust me these 2 strategies will definitely work as I have tested them for a year and built www.wharfstreetstrategies.com and www.wharfstreetstudios.com which is again amazing. That's what positive energy does and when you open your mind, you will definitely experience it.

Now let me share the best part of my experience as a gift to you and I am sure this will blow your mind:

Energy Flow Quadrant, this explains the way in which energy flows over time impacting the growth in our life. If the flow of energy is in the right direction then it will help achieve goals in life with ease. In simple words, some call it a "Miracle", but honestly the ideal flow is to channelise energy at the right time on different levels. The flow of energy can be in many ways it could be through people, through money and knowledge as well. And trust me this energy impacts one's life based on their willingness to share knowledge, experience, abilities, talent, skills and expertise which are termed as "gifts". Growth in Life according to this quadrant progresses alongside with time.

ENERGY FLOW QUADRANT Diagram

G **GIFTS** YOU ARE STAGNANT 🎁 → 👤	M **MONEY** YOU BUILD NETWORTH 🎁 → 💵
P **PEOPLE** YOU SIMPLY NETWORK 🎁 → 👥	I **INTELLECT** YOU SHARE KNOWLEDGE 🎁 → 👤

In the first quadrant all your gifts are usually not shared and kept to yourself. Energy becomes **Stagnant** with time. Here, time is spent in one's comfort zone and there is no multiplication in any form, unknowingly one stays selfish or self-centered.

In the second quadrant one enhances his/her talent to acquire skills by sharing gifts through interaction. Here, energy is multiplied through networking and increasing your contact list. One's skills and energy flow will be directly proportional to his acquired network and environment at that moment. Energy becomes **Social** with time.

In the third quadrant, increase in skill sets due to interaction urges the need for commercialising the gifts. This further can lead to a valuation in the market as gifts are monetised and energy shared is proportional to money. Energy could become **Fame** with time and later lead to branding as well.

In the final quadrant knowledge and energy are shared without expectation, so there is no boundary and energy flow is free and more in multiplication. Here energy becomes **Wisdom** over time and one can become an enlightened intellect.

Basically energy increases from 1st quadrant to the last and based on the quadrant there is growth over time.

4 Stages of Energy Flow Quadrant

All stages have distinct attributes in one's life and each quadrant represents a different energy level. One can maximise energy by moving through these stages one step after the other. These stages can be measured in terms of Growth vs Time:

Stage 1: *No time, No growth*

When you read, travel and interact your gifts will get enlightened deep inside enhancing your skill set and expertise, making you knowledgeable. Keeping these gifts with oneself, makes them stagnant without any energy multiplying.

Stage 2: *Some time, Some growth*

When you start connecting with people by networking and interacting, thereby sharing knowledge, your gifts multiply and will be proportional to your contacts in an environment.

Stage 3: *Enough time, Enough growth*

When one's focus is money, these gifts can be commercialised wherein gifts are exchanged for money. This increases one's net worth and could possibly create a valuation for them in the market.

Stage 4: *Substantial time, Substantial growth*

Sharing these gifts without any expectation only for the benefit of millennials and betterment of this world gives you the experience of being an enlightened one. Again your knowledge multiplies as you share it without materialistic expectations.

One utilises his/her energy to traverse these stages and progress to the next levels of the quadrant.

ENERGY FLOW in my case

1. No Multiplication: Eclerx (2015-2016)
2. Multiplication of people: Events in UK (2017)
3. Multiplication of Money: Various Start-up (2018)

4. Multiplication of knowledge: Founded Wharf Street Strategies (www.wharfstreetstrategies.com) without any expectation (2019)

Towards the end of this book, at this moment I would like to express sincere gratitude to family. Apart from differences with parents at some low points in life. I would still like to honour them with the credit for supporting me and inspiring me always with their doings. Parents didn't have good education due to their circumstances. Grandfather expired when father was 13 years old. Right now father is a Commercial Assistant in the French Embassy (Oman) for 40 years. Mother hailed from a village and now is a Property Landlord in India. They are both financially successful to this date with their efforts, previously doing all odd jobs and their sacrifices to get to this point.

I had all the education but simply felt that I was stuck in the rat race and if parents scaled that way without proper education and support. I should definitely leverage on education, knowledge and support from family to make life worthy for this planet. Lo! I am here completing this book right after successfully building two companies.

The takeaway from this chapter is "Never forget what and where you were when you started". This acknowledgment itself brings a solution to many problems in life, when you scale up your mind might channelise and lead to situations where you forget who you actually are.

Also if you have learnt enough from this book and are rich enough then instead of donating food and money to charities. Kindly share this knowledge as this is the best charity which would change lives to make a difference to this planet.

I would also like to express sincere gratitude to chief Operations Officer, **Aniket Bhosale** and Chief Marketing Officer ,**Sonali Bansal** for helping me complete this book.

As this is the last chapter i really hope and wish that your time has proven to be worthwhile with me as I believe that all stories, strategies and mind-boggling concepts in this book have added value in your life in some form or the other.

APPENDIX

I always dreamt to live, study & explore this planet to the fullest and would love to share this journey & experiences with other people. I have pursued engineering from the prestigious Vellore Institute of Technology, Vellore & then got an opportunity to work with TCS as Assistant System Engineer. After a couple of years at TCS, I wanted to broaden my perspective of a business or corporate world. I got an opportunity to do masters at Amity University, Delhi. I personally believe, an MBA degree does not only help the students to become better entrepreneurs or managers but also help them with leadership qualities, the courage to take risks, experiment & adapt to a new culture or situations. Also, I have sound knowledge and expertise in Banking and Finance, Operations, IT sector with an expertise in the field of management and hold experience with Top 5 US- based Investment Banks.

Later I moved out of India to London and successfully completed the course at Anglia Ruskin University with an M.Sc. in Supply Chain Management along with the Bloomberg Terminal certification. Further finished internship, wherein I have been working towards building some of today's most exciting Fintech, Social media, Gaming, Technology and Service business.

At this point I was engrossed in multiple projects, playing a lead role making me seek further opportunities in career growth. Apart from previous experience in the investment banking sector, I expanded rapidly in various fields required to create two companies. To sum up, motto is to dedicatedly implement all the knowledge I have been acquiring over the years.

As I have been involved in various projects based on emerging technologies like Blockchain, Machine Learning and Artificial Intelligence and emerging marketing techniques with unique tools. This has helped me to develop personality as a multitasker and I have learned to cope with pressure. For me every task and activity is important and I justify everything I do. Aim is not only to raise myself but also to help grow team, clients and contribute to this planet in the best possible way.

Printed in Great Britain
by Amazon